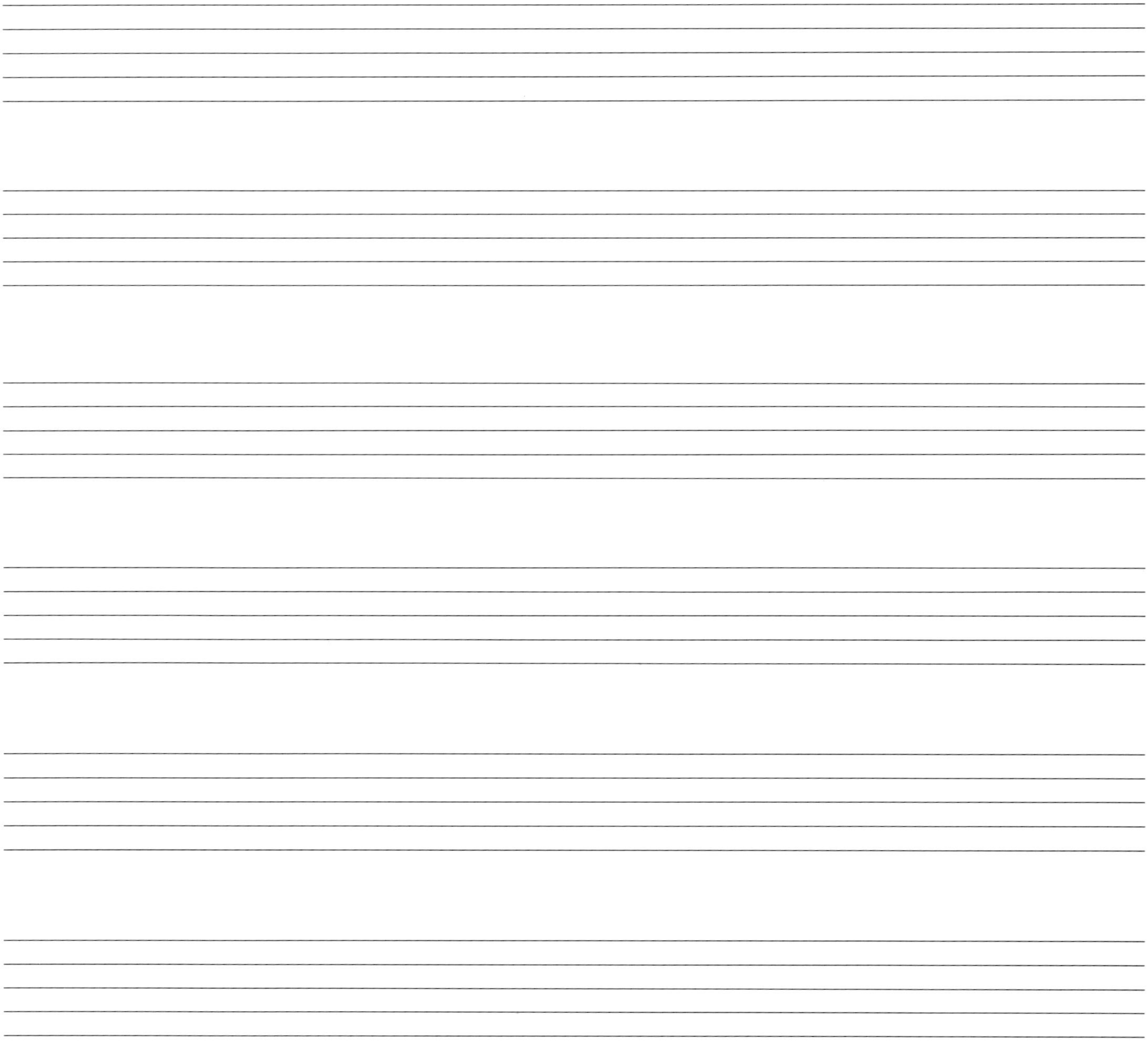

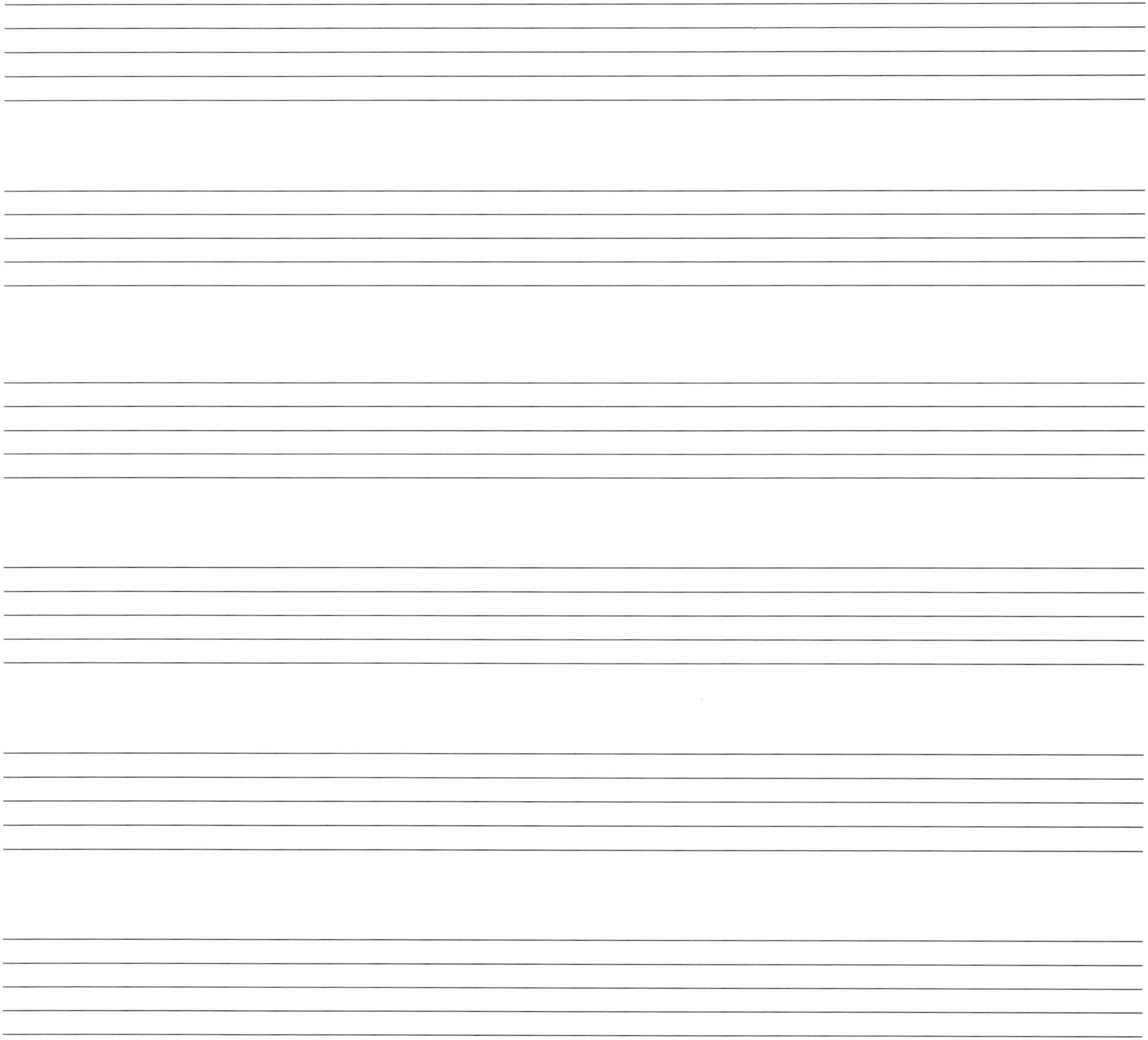

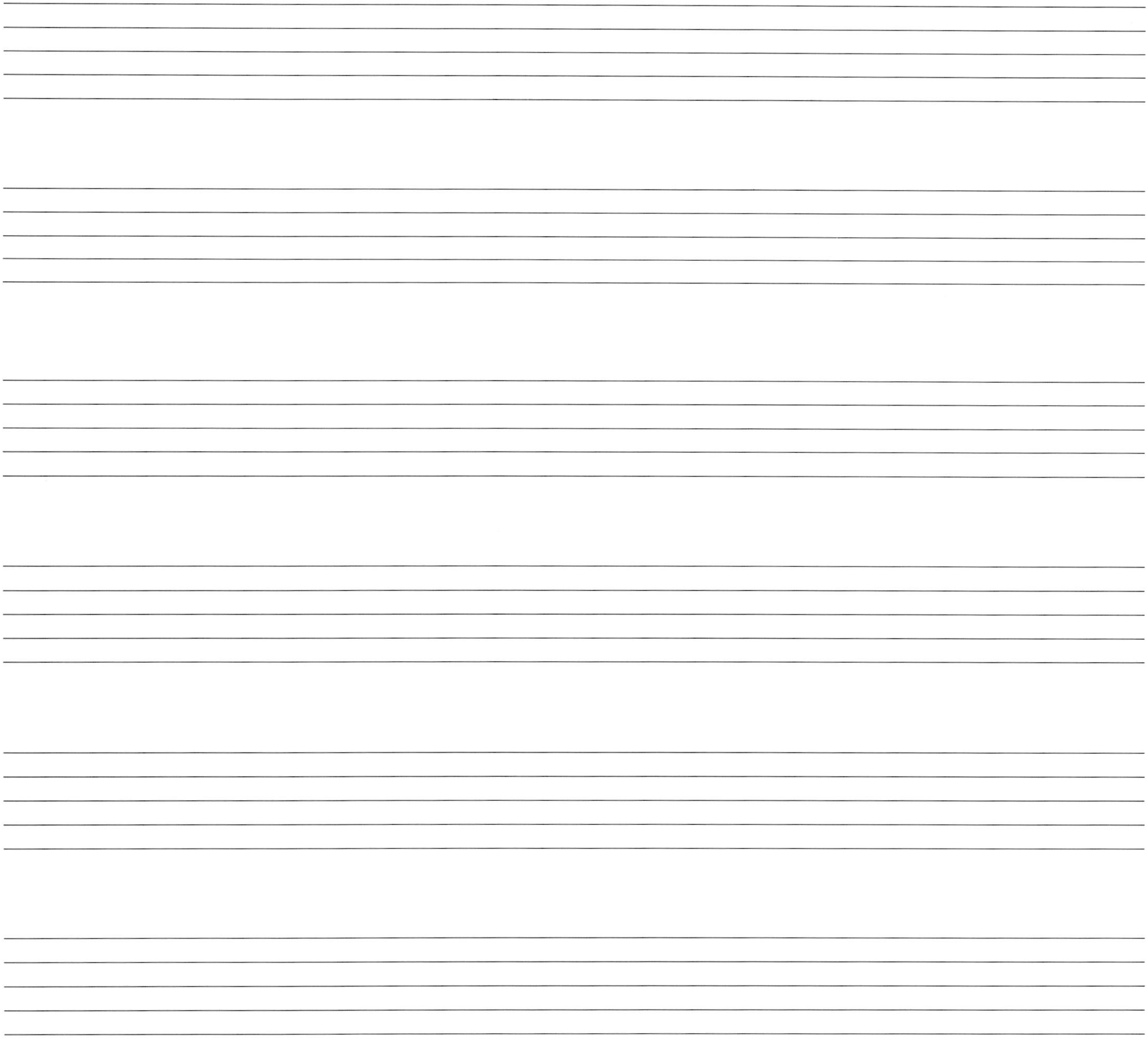

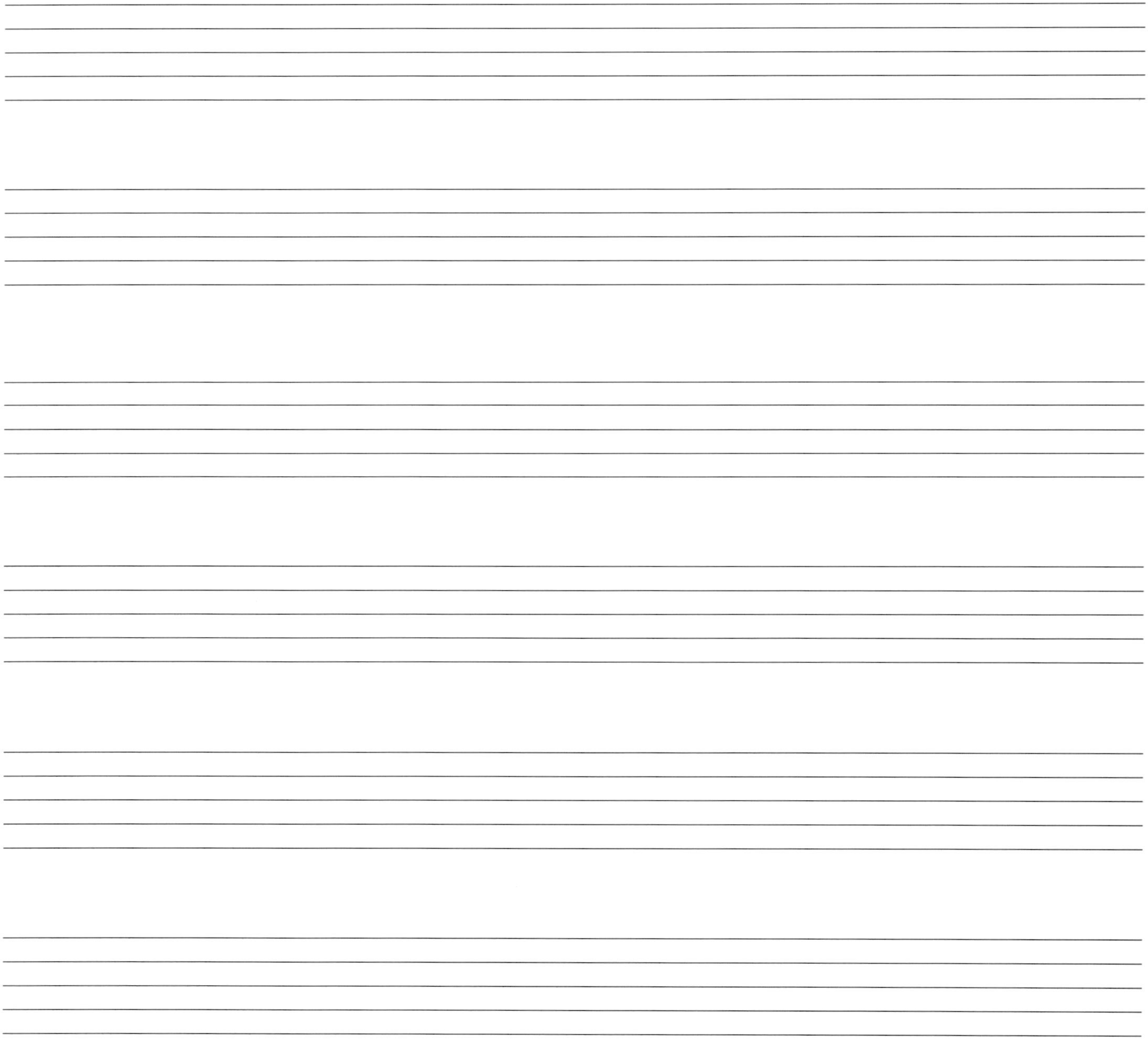

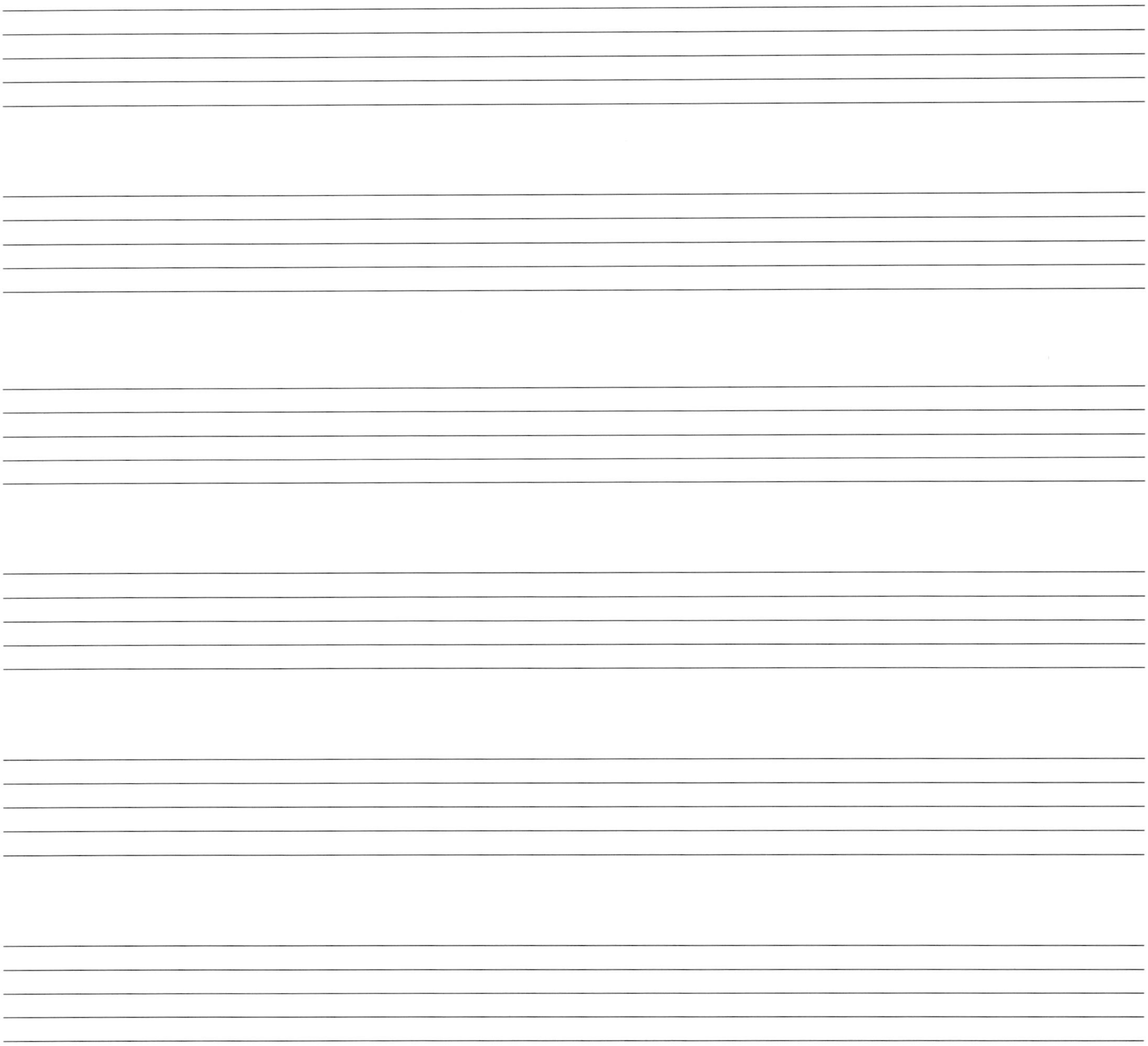

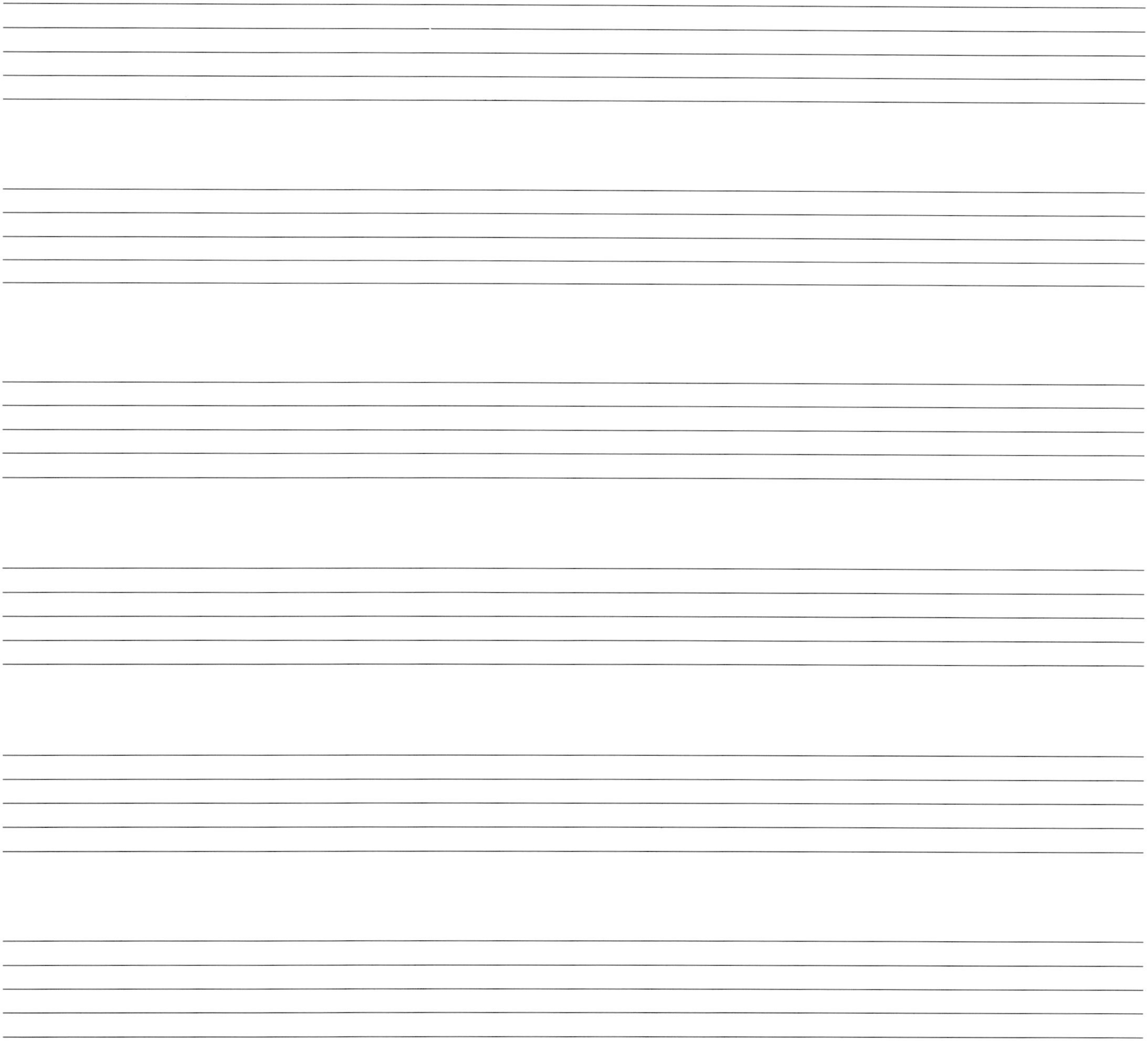

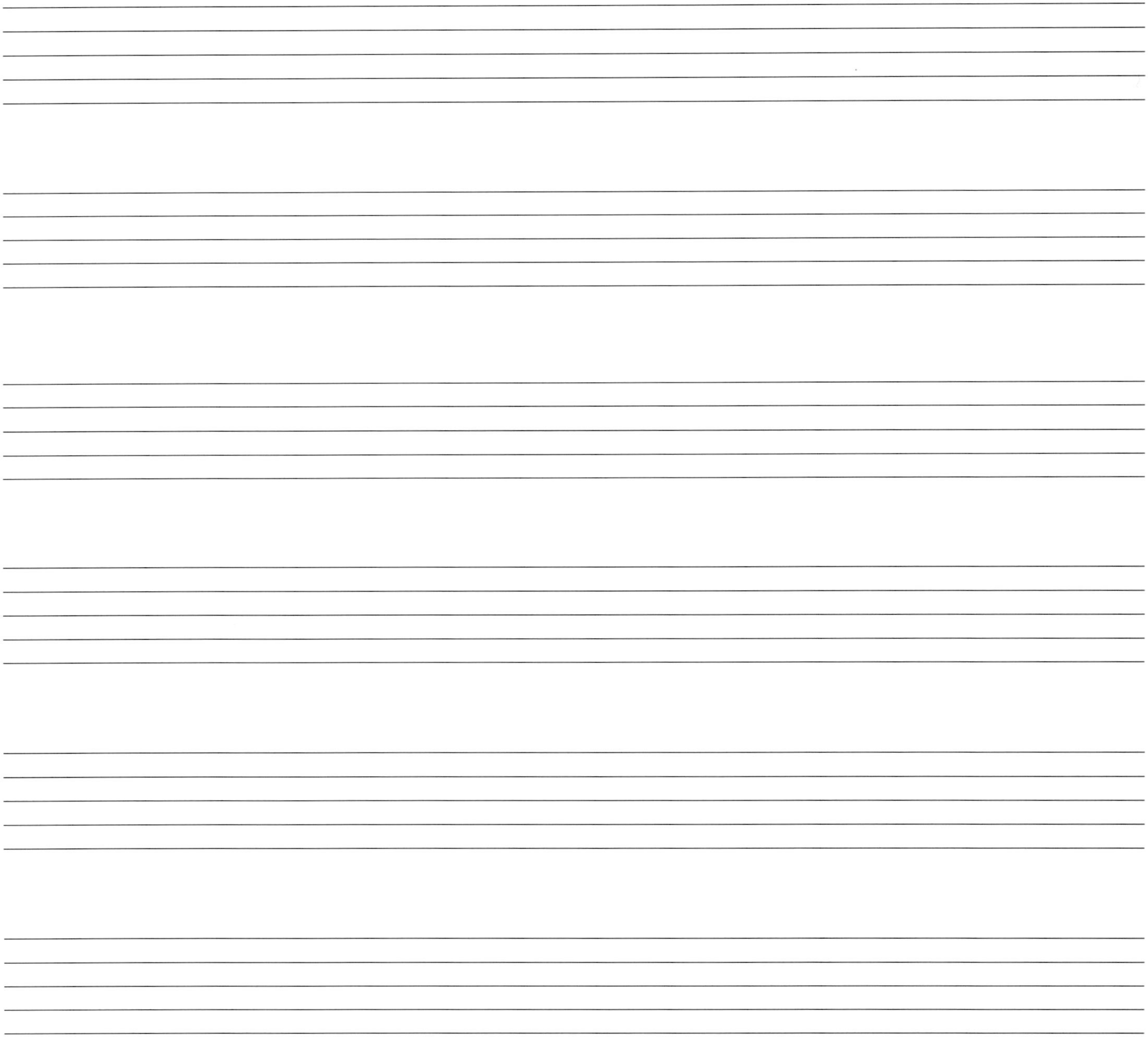

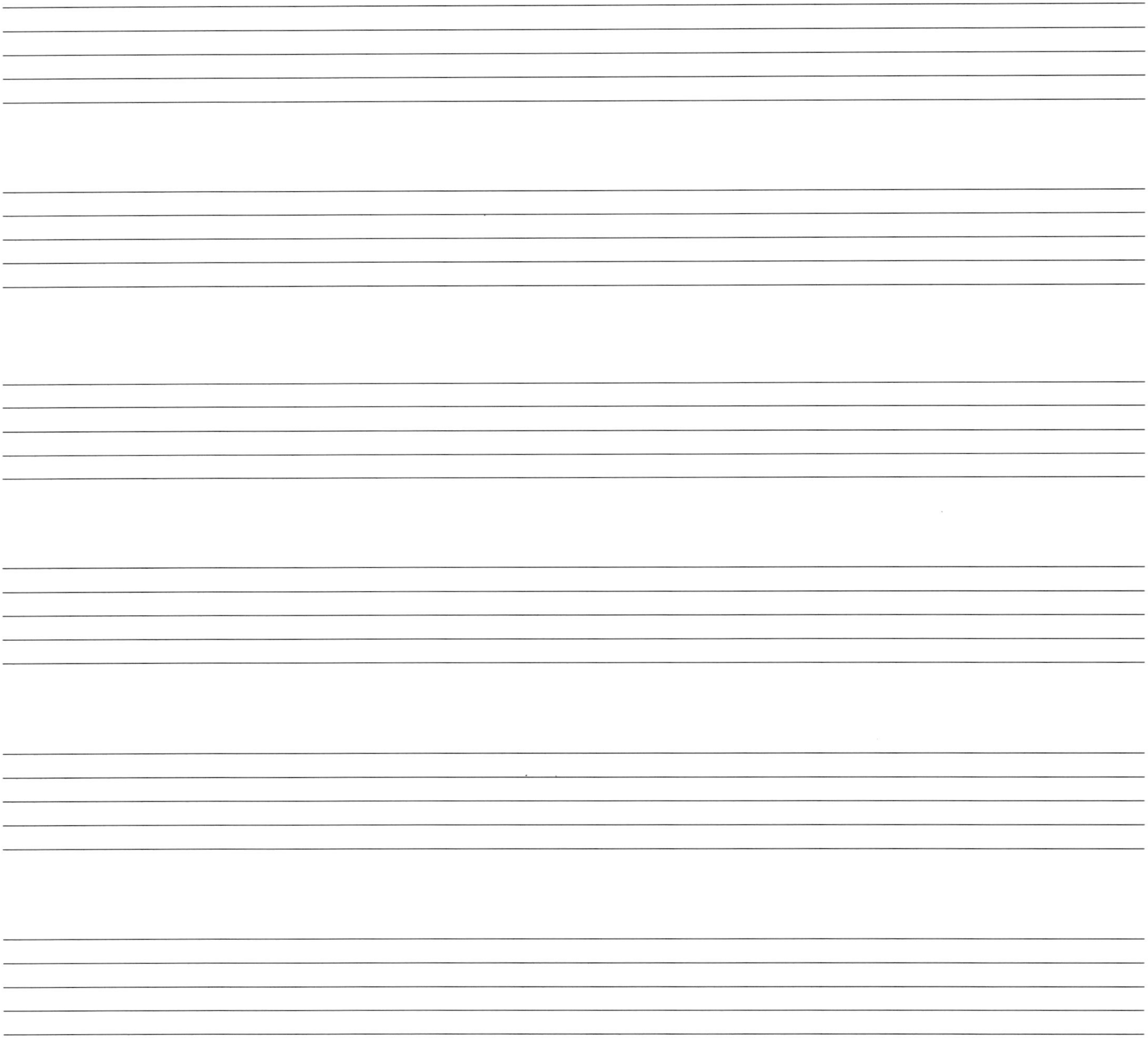

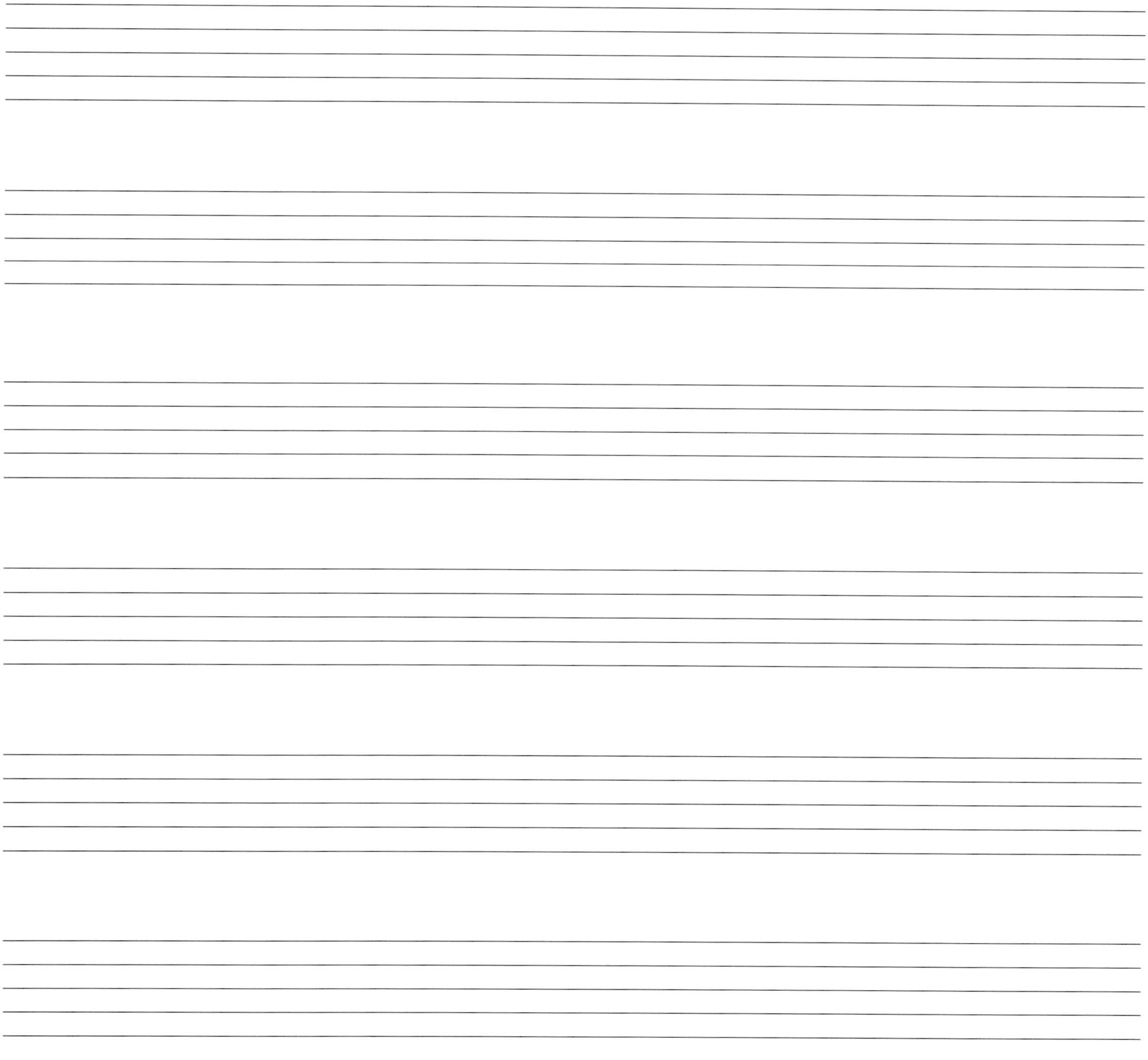

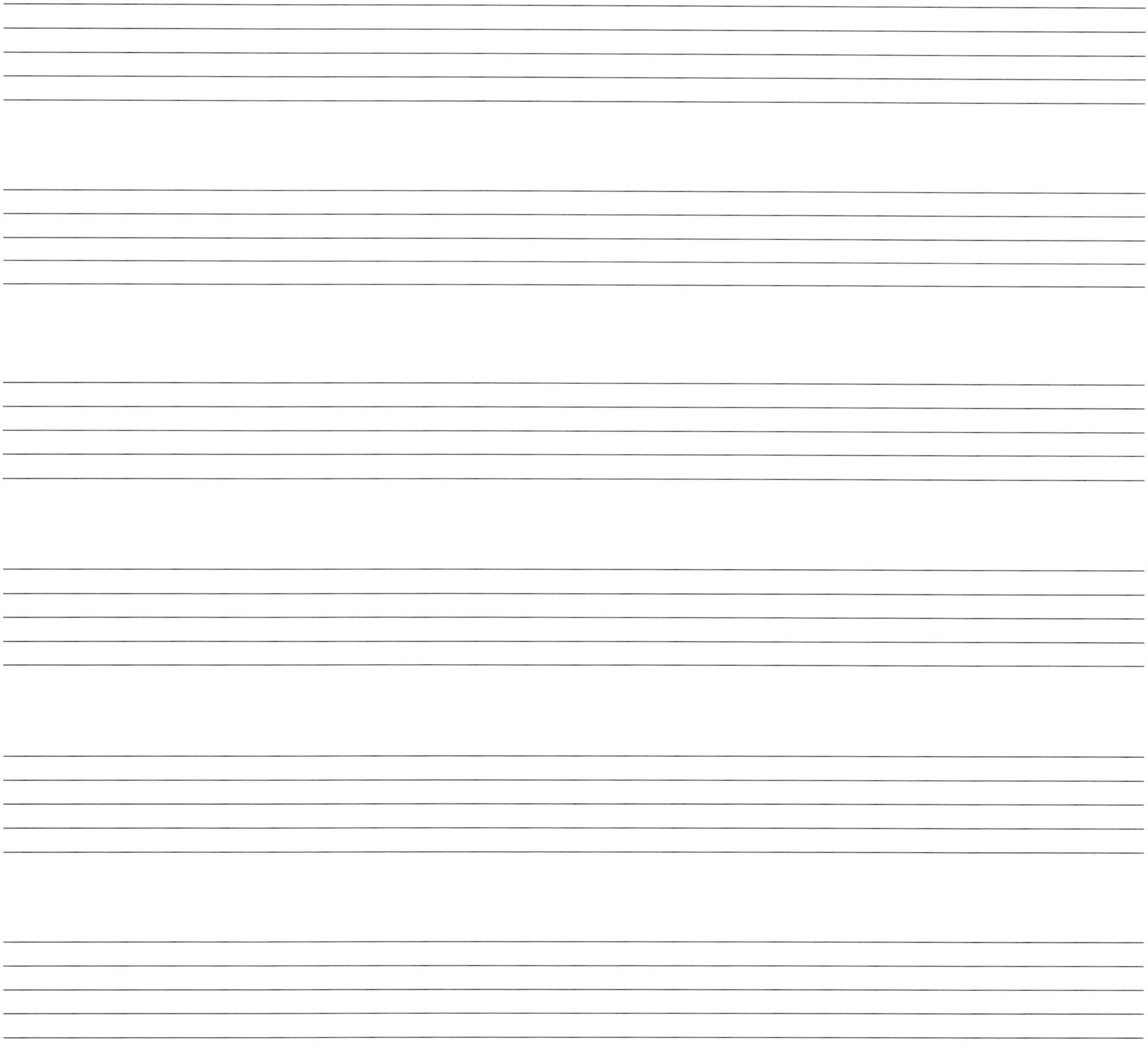

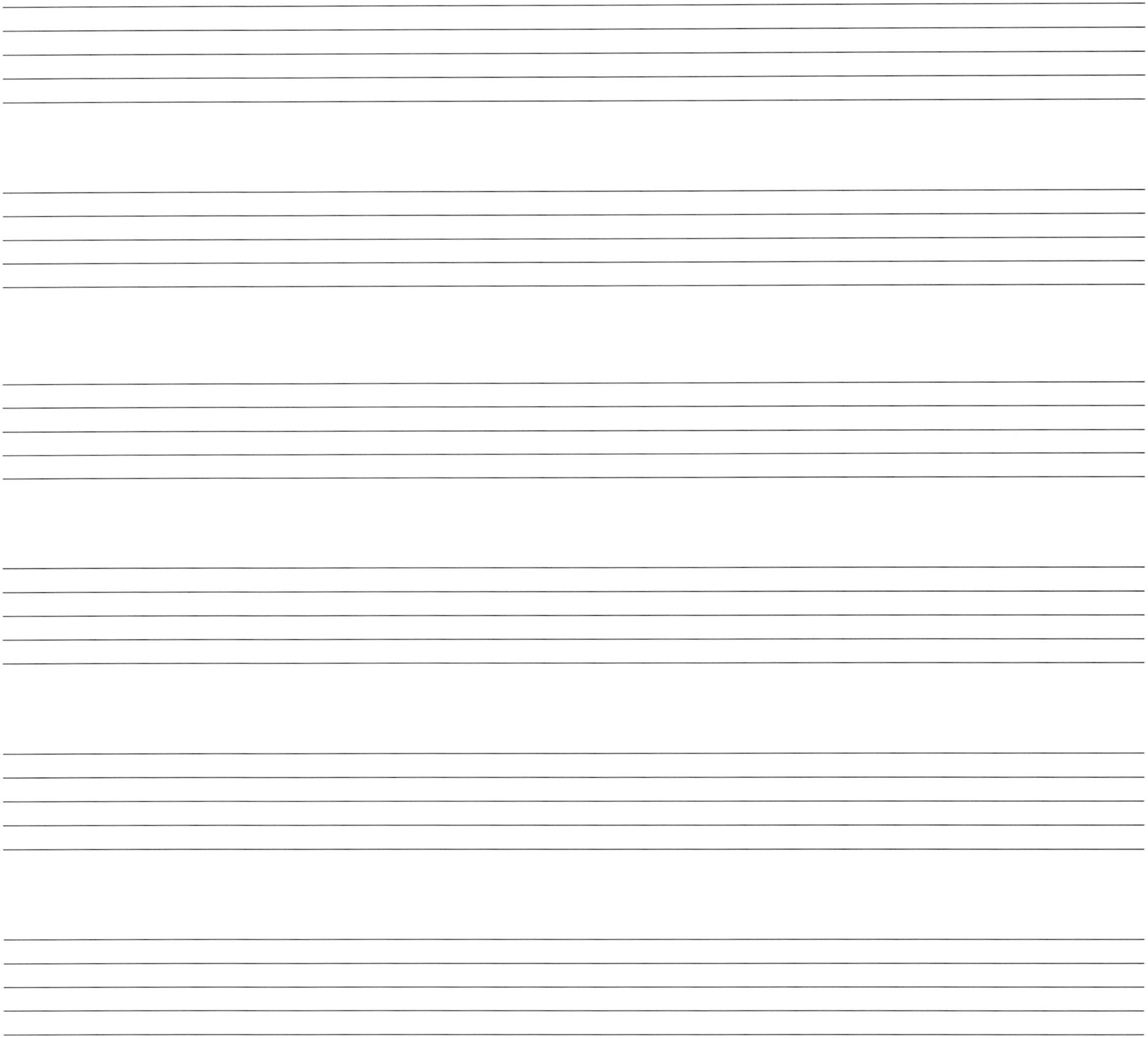

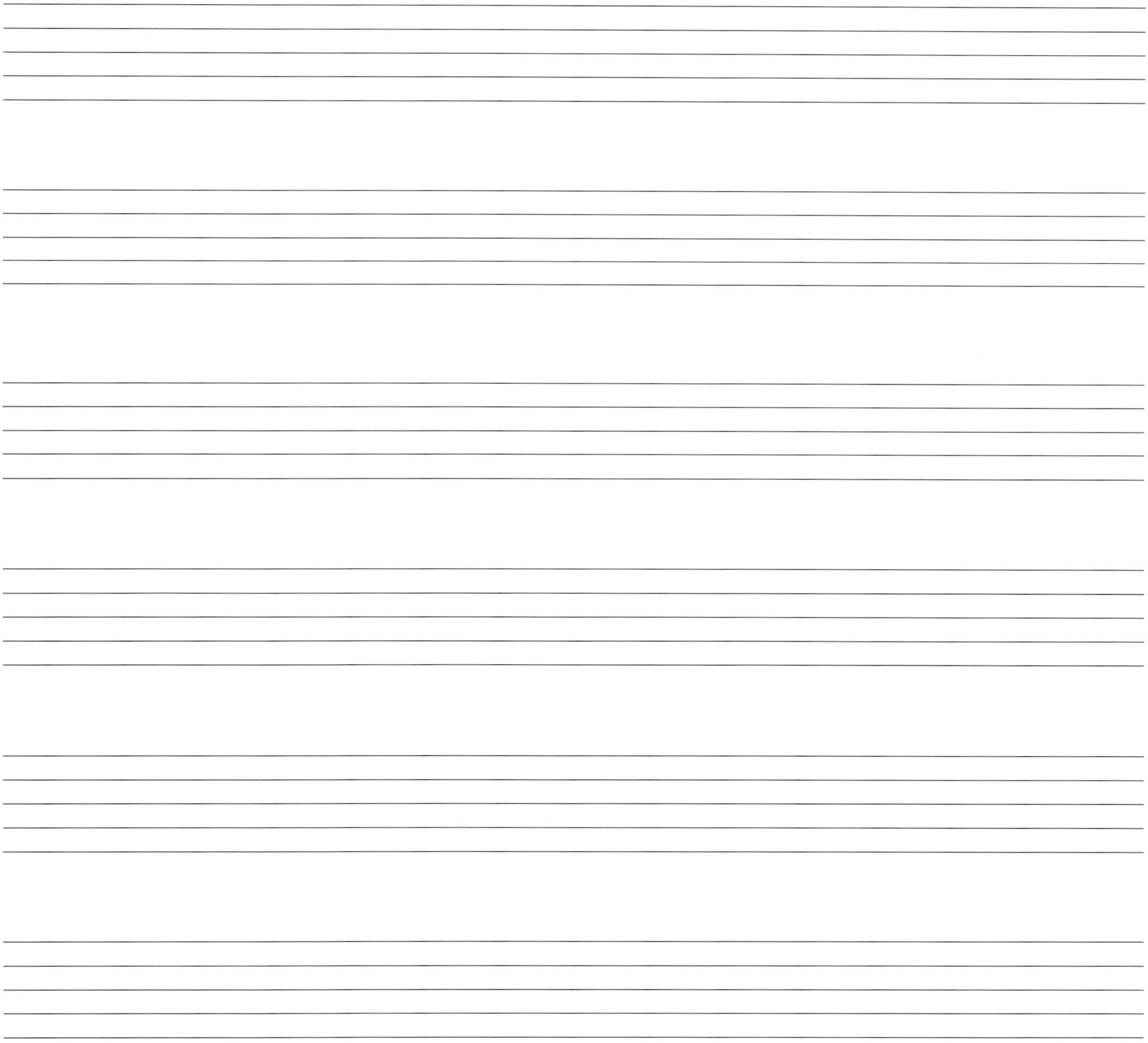

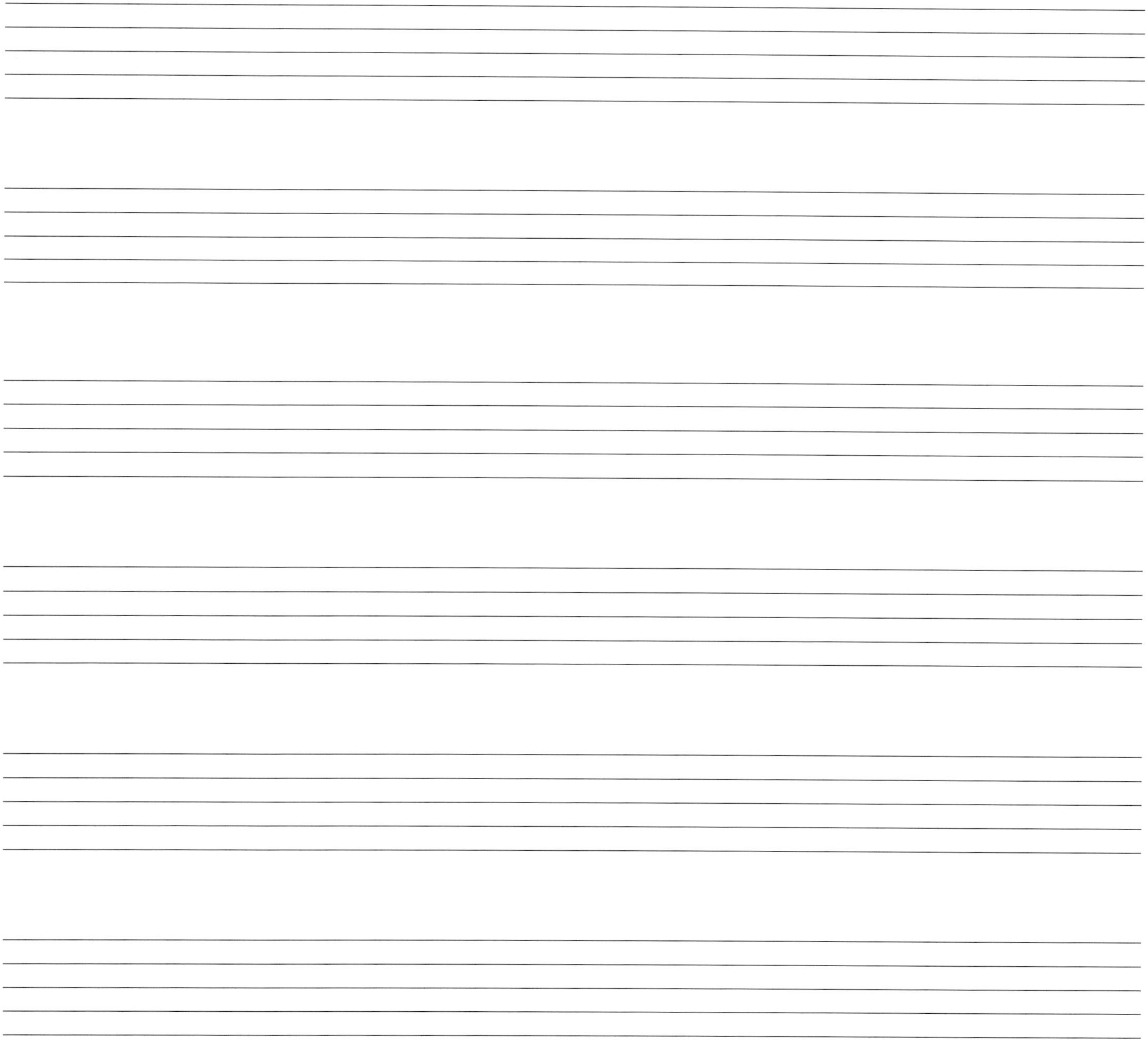

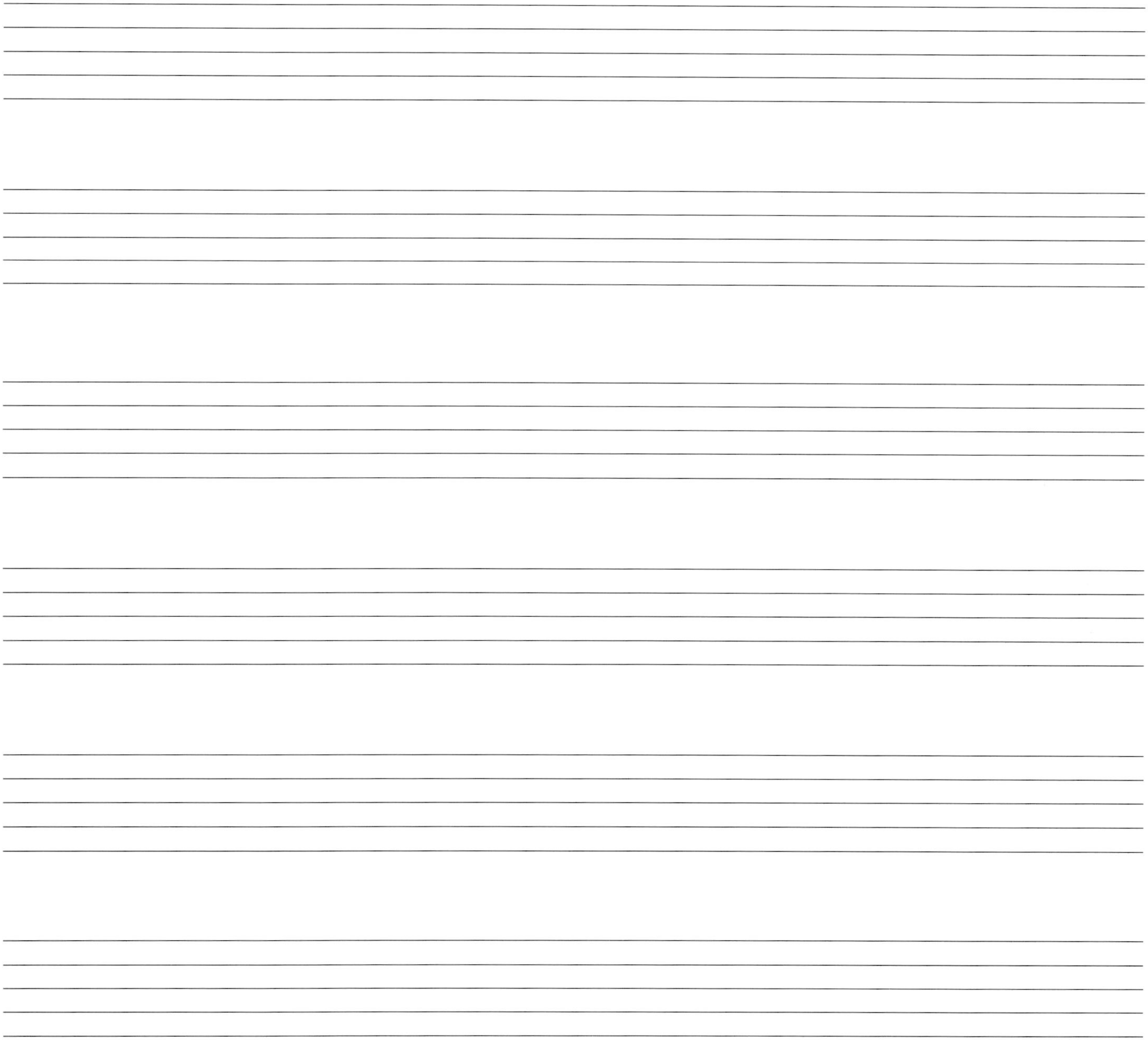

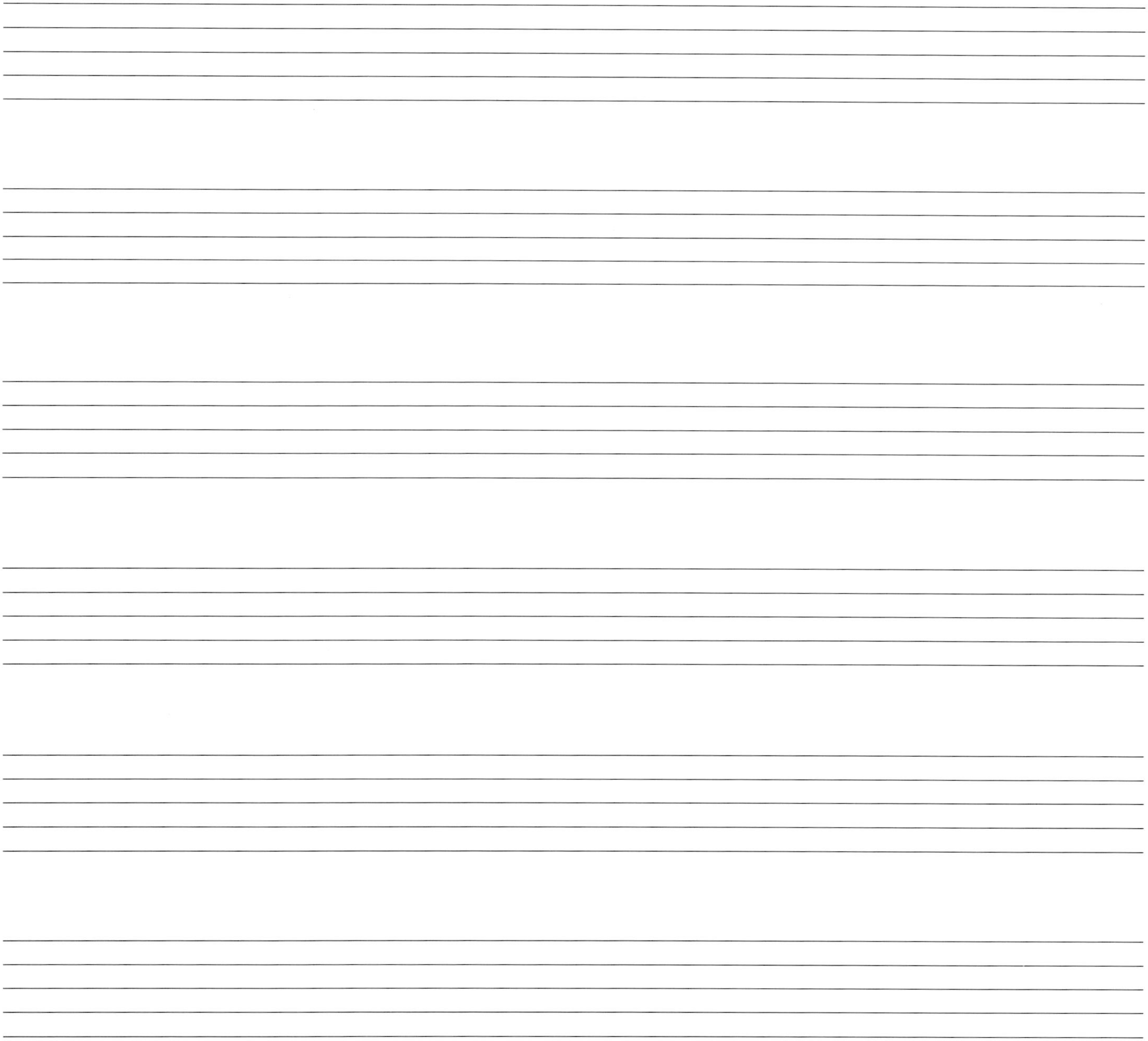

Printed in Great
Britain
by Amazon

31249111R00025